ORGAN
Gospel Treasures

ISBN 978-1-4950-1780-3

HAL•LEONARD® CORPORATION

7777 W. BLUEMOUND RD. P.O. BOX 13819 MILWAUKEE, WI 53213

In Australia Contact:
Hal Leonard Australia Pty. Ltd.
4 Lentara Court
Cheltenham, Victoria, 3192 Australia
Email: ausadmin@halleonard.com.au

Visit Hal Leonard Online at
www.halleonard.com

Amazing Grace

Registration 13

Words by John Newton
Traditional American Melody

Are You Washed in the Blood?

Registration 7

Words and Music by
Elisha A. Hoffman

At Calvary

Registration 2

Words by William R. Newell
Music by Daniel B. Towner

Blessed Assurance

Registration 16

Lyrics by Fanny J. Crosby
Music by Phoebe Palmer Knapp

Beautiful Isle of Somewhere

Registration 5

Words by Jessie B. Pounds
Music by John S. Fearis

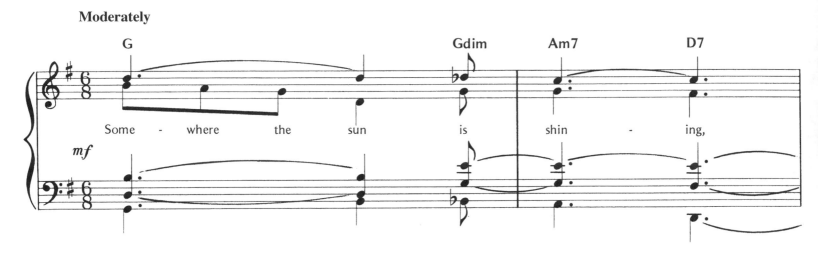

Some - where the sun is shin - ing,

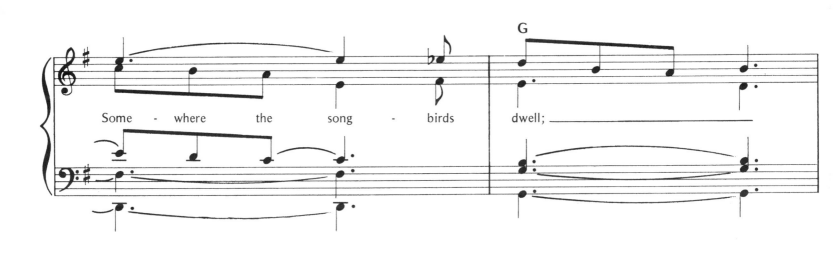

Some - where the song - birds dwell;

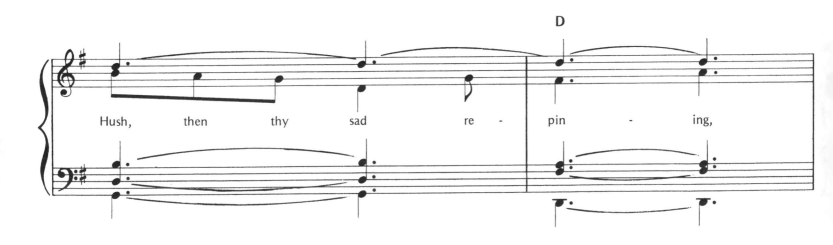

Hush, then thy sad re - pin - ing,

Bringing in the Sheaves

Registration 2

Words by Knowles Shaw
Music by George A. Minor

Church in the Wildwood

Registration 12

Words and Music by
Dr. William S. Pitts

Down at the Cross
(Glory to His Name)

Registration 3

Words by Elisha A. Hoffman
Music by John H. Stockton

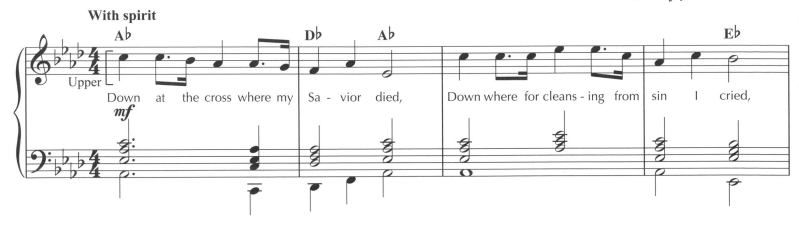

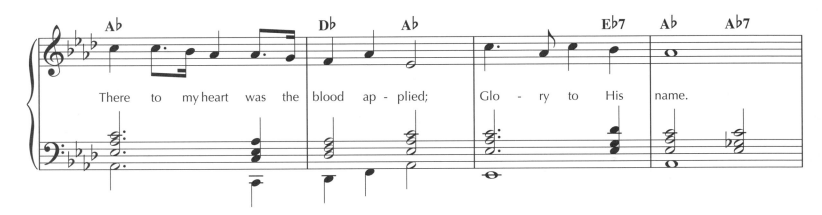

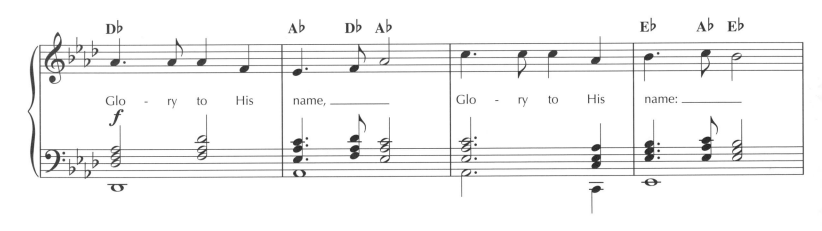

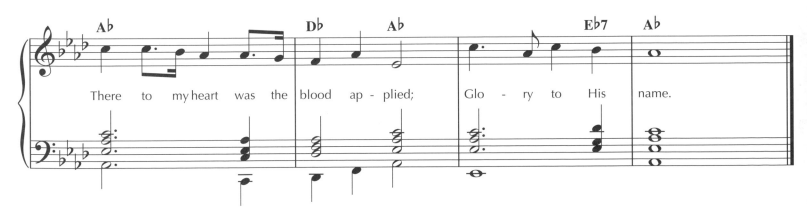

Higher Ground

Registration 3

Words by Johnson Oatman, Jr.
Music by Charles H. Gabriel

I Love to Tell the Story

Registration 16

Words by A. Catherine Hankey
Music by William G. Fischer

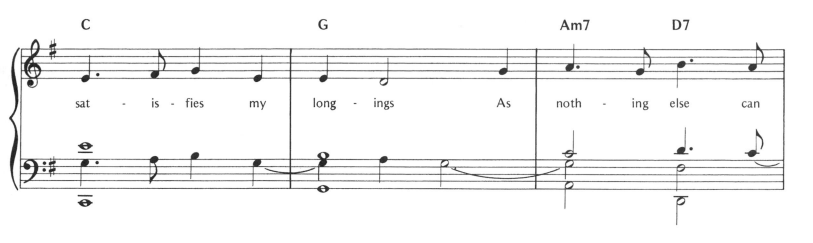

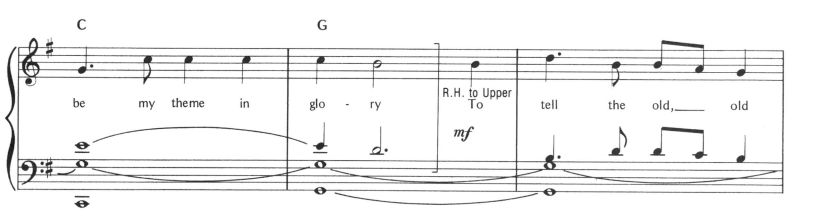

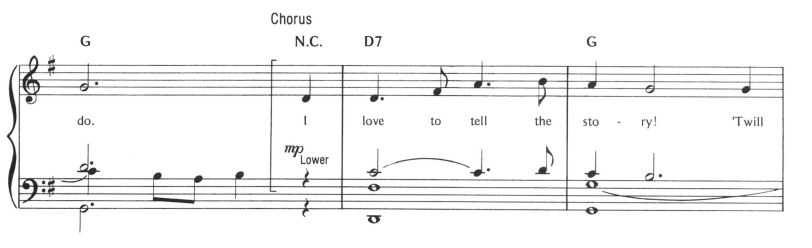

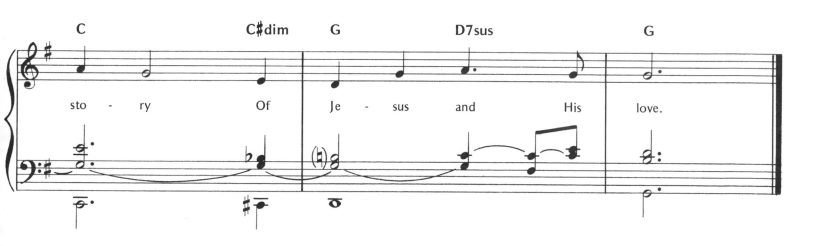

I Surrender All

Registration 18

Words by J.W. Van Deventer
Music by W.S. Weeden

In the Garden

Registration 12

Words and Music by
C. Austin Miles

Jesus Saves!

Registration 2

Words by Priscilla J. Owens
Music by William J. Kirkpatrick

Just As I Am

Registration 15

Words by Charlotte Elliott
Music by William B. Bradbury

Just a Closer Walk with Thee

Registration 15

Traditional
Arranged by Kenneth Morris

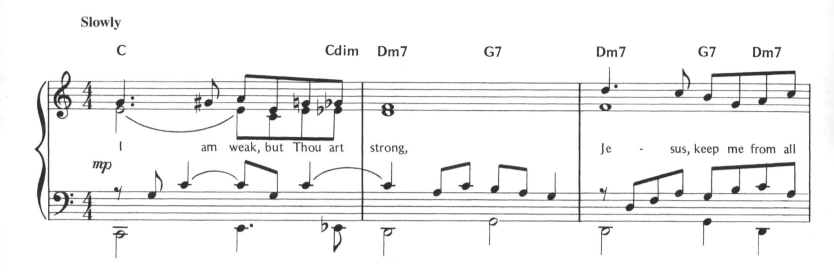

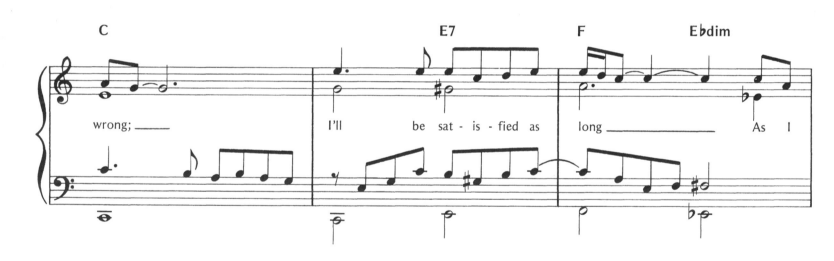

Leaning on the Everlasting Arms

Registration 8

Words by Elisha A. Hoffman
Music by Anthony J. Showalter

Nearer, My God, to Thee

Registration 18

Words by Sarah F. Adams
Based on Genesis 28:10–22
Music by Lowell Mason

Nothing But the Blood

Registration 2

Words and Music by
Robert Lowry

The Old Rugged Cross

Registration 8

Words and Music by
Rev. George Bennard

Only Trust Him

Registration 1

Words and Music by
John H. Stockton

Pass Me Not, O Gentle Savior

Registration 8

Words by Fanny J. Crosby
Music by William H. Doane

Precious Memories

Registration 15

Words and Music by
J.B.F. Wright

Revive Us Again

Registration 11

Words by William P. MacKay
Music by John J. Husband

Rock of Ages

Registration 5

Words by Augustus M. Toplady
Music by Thomas Hastings

Savior, Like a Shepherd Lead Us

Registration 8

Words from *Hymns for the Young*
Attributed to Dorothy A. Thrupp
Music by William B. Bradbury

Shall We Gather at the River?

Registration 11

Words and Music by
Robert Lowry

Standing on the Promises

Registration 3

Words and Music by
R. Kelso Carter

Sweet By and By

Registration 7

Words by Sanford Fillmore Bennett
Music by Joseph P. Webster

Moderately

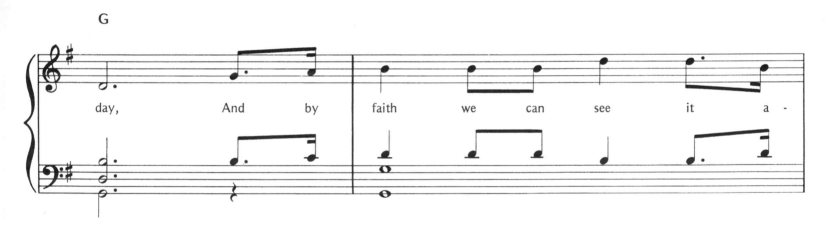

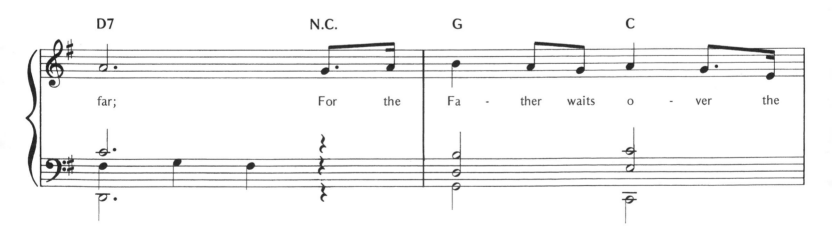

Sweet Hour of Prayer

Registration 17

Words by William W. Walford
Music by William B. Bradbury

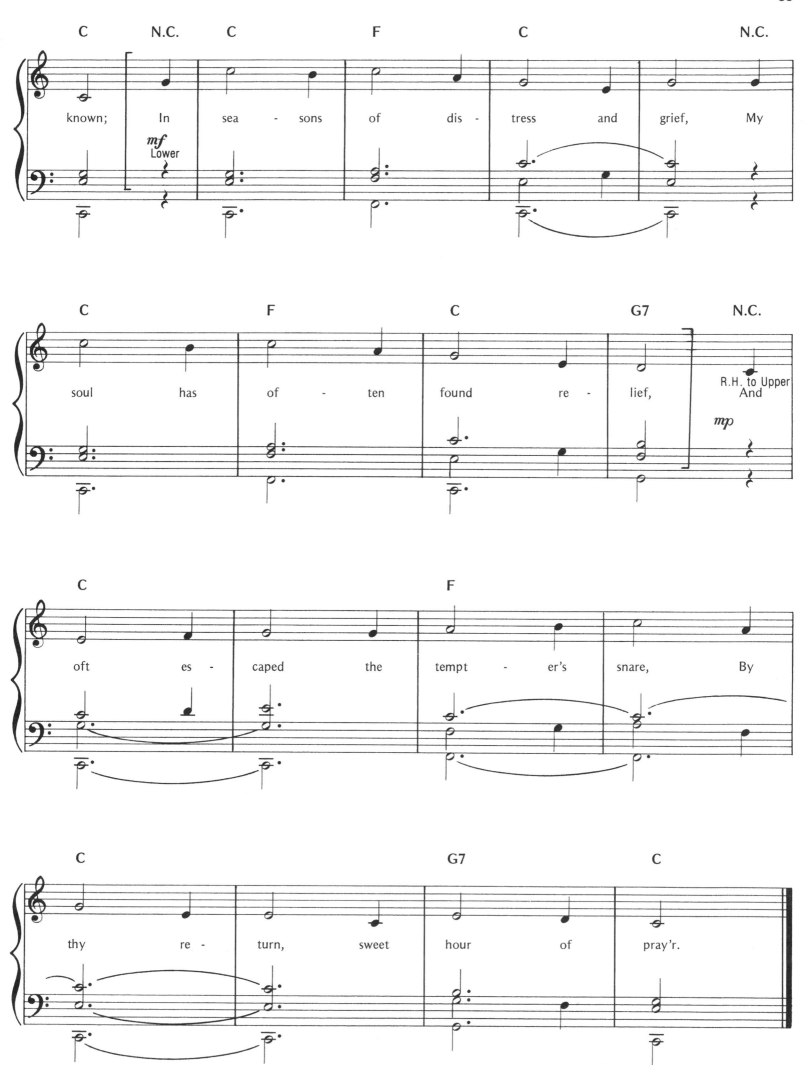

Trust and Obey

Registration 12

Words by John H. Sammis
Music by Daniel B. Towner

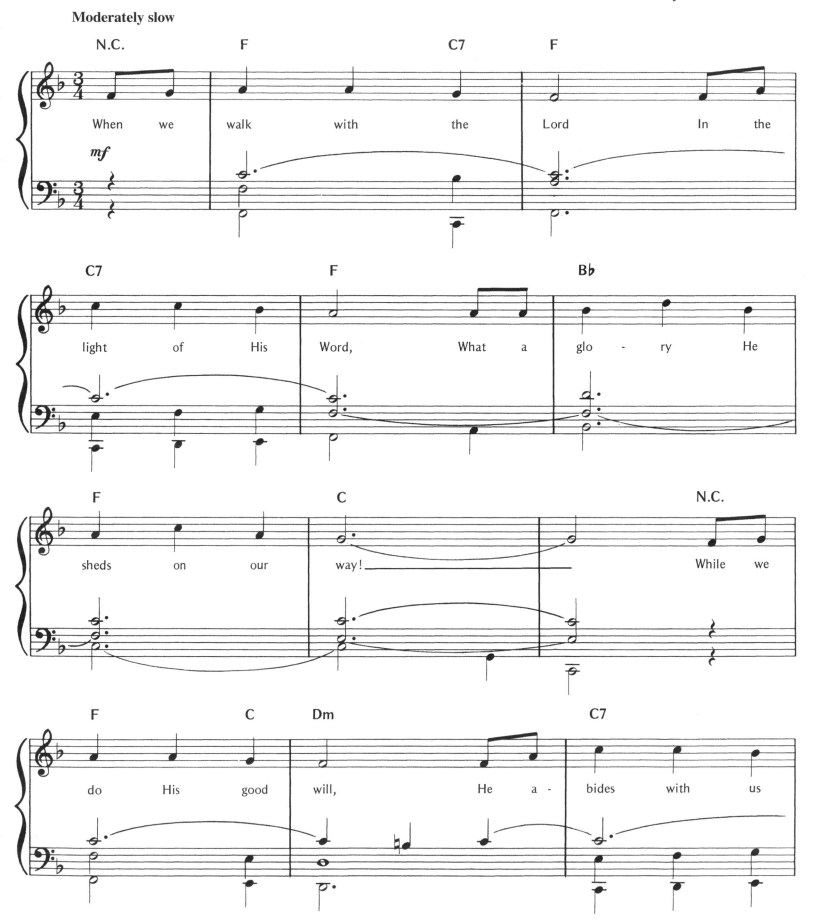

What a Friend We Have in Jesus

Registration 4

Words by Joseph M. Scriven
Music by Charles C. Converse

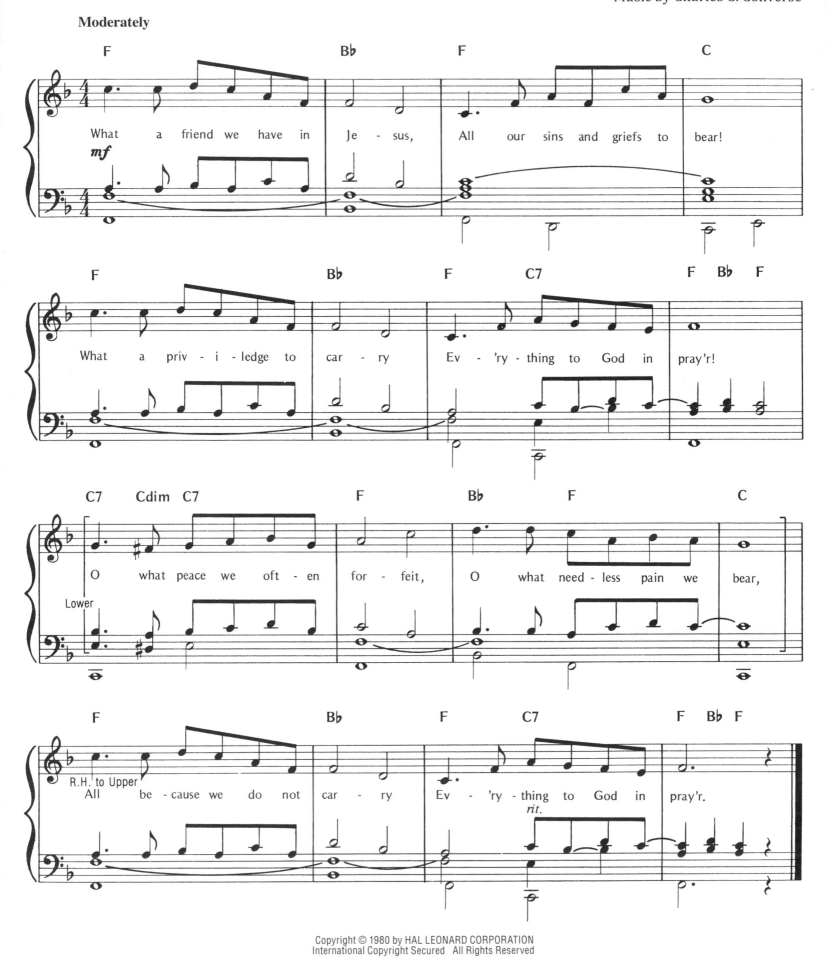

When We All Get to Heaven

Registration 2

Words by Eliza E. Hewitt
Music by Emily D. Wilson

When the Roll Is Called Up Yonder

Registration 2

Words and Music by
James M. Black

Moderately, with spirit

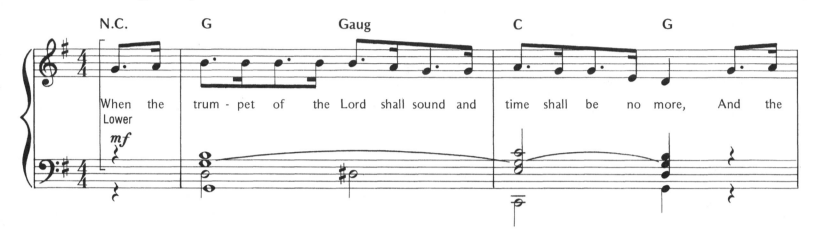

When the trum-pet of the Lord shall sound and time shall be no more, And the

Lower

_mf_

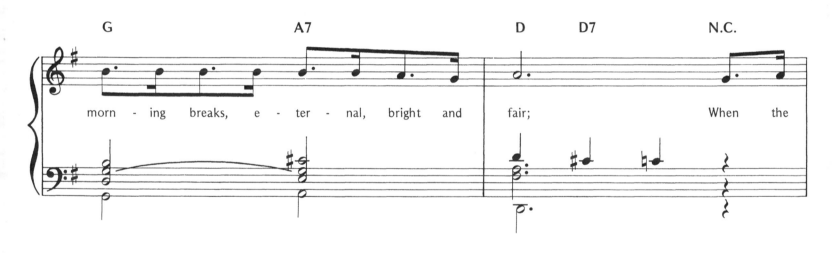

morn - ing breaks, e - ter - nal, bright and fair; When the

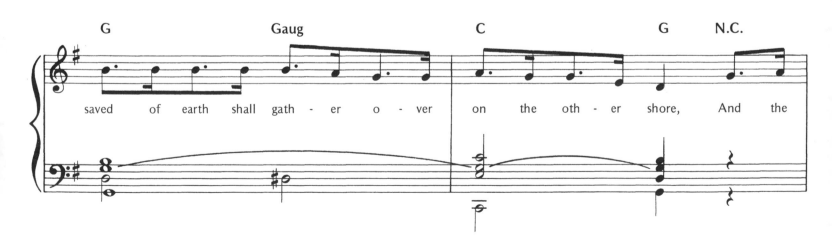

saved of earth shall gath - er o - ver on the oth - er shore, And the

Whispering Hope

Registration 1

Words and Music by
Alice Hawthorne

Wonderful Peace

Registration 8

Words by W.D. Cornell
Music by W.G. Cooper

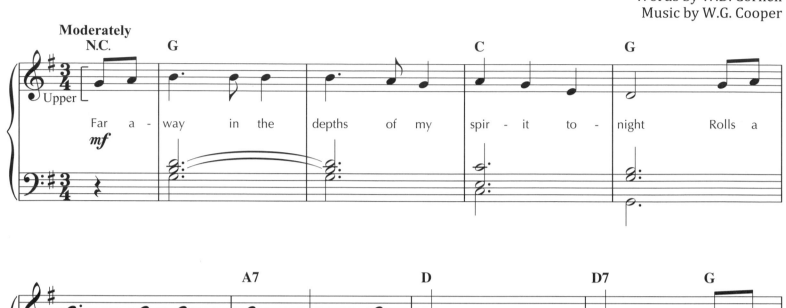

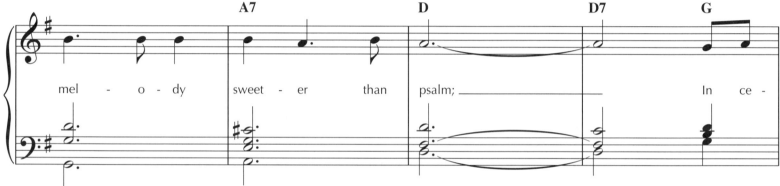

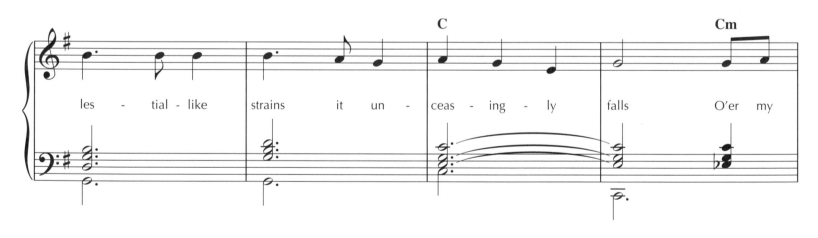

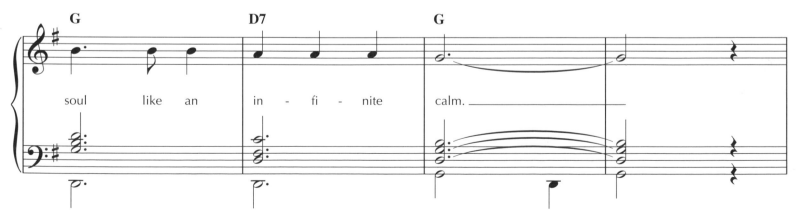

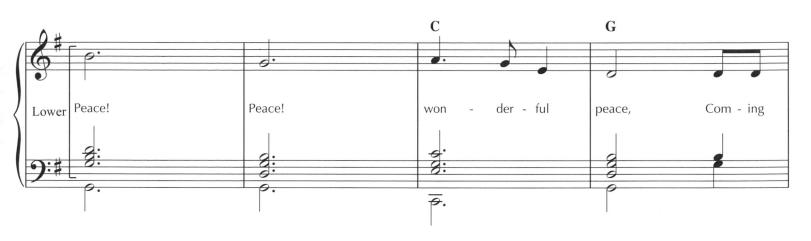

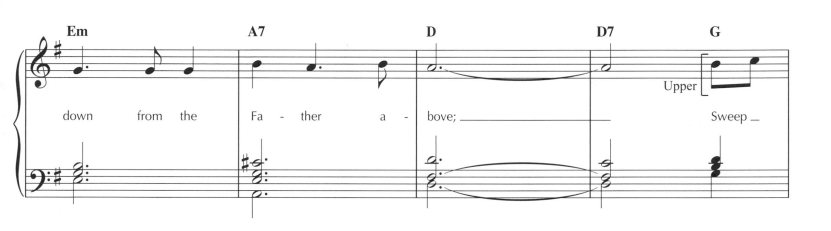

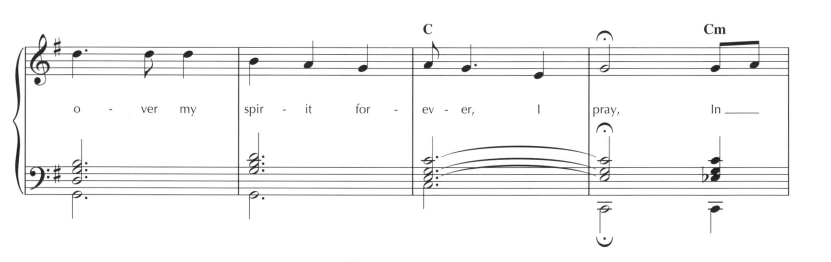

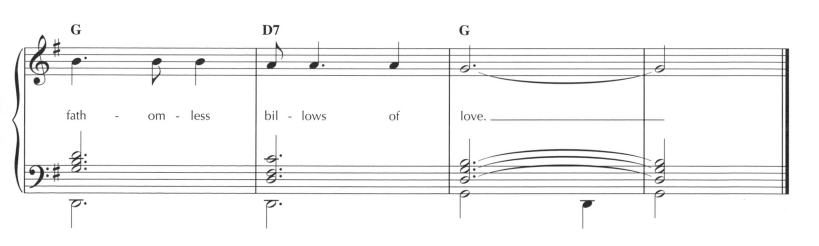

REGISTRATION CHART

Each numbered registration will produce a different sound. Match the number on the song to the same number on this chart; then engage the organ voices and controls as indicated.

1
Electronic Organs
Upper: Flute (or Tibia) 16'
(or Bassoon 16'),
Reed 8', String 4'
Lower: Flutes 8', 4', String 8'
Pedal: 16', 8' Medium Loud
Vib./Trem.: On, Full (Opt. Off)

Tonebar Organs
Upper: 88 0080 660
Lower: (00) 7755 422
Pedal: 65
Vib./Trem.: On, Full (Opt. Off)

11
Electronic Organs
Upper: Full Organ 8', 4', 2', 1'
Lower: Flute 8', String 4', Reed 4'
Pedal: 16', 8' Medium
Vib./Trem.: On, Full (Opt. Off)

Tonebar Organs
Upper: 00 8558 446
Lower: (00) 6644 232
Pedal: 55
Vib./Trem.: On, Full (Opt. Off)

2
Electronic Organs
Upper: Full Organ 16', 8', 4', 2', 1'
(Use Strings 8', 4')
Lower: Diapason 8',
Flutes 8', 4', 2',
String 8', Reed 4'
Pedal: 16', 8'
Medium Loud/Sustain
Vib./Trem.: On, Full

Tonebar Organs
Upper: 60 8586 666
Lower: (00) 7764 443
Pedal: 56 String Bass
Vib./Trem.: On, Full

12
Electronic Organs
Upper: Flute (or Tibia) 4',
Reed 8'
Lower: Diapason 8'
Pedal: 16', 8' Medium
Vib./Trem.: On, Small

Tonebar Organs
Upper: 00 6886 080
Lower: (00) 7633 323
Pedal: 54
Vib./Trem.: On, Small

3
Electronic Organs
Upper: Trumpet (or Brass) 8'
Lower: Diapason 8'
Pedal: 16', 8' Medium
Vib./Trem.: On, Small (Opt. Off)

Tonebar Organs
Upper: 00 6787 654
Lower: (00) 6543 221
Pedal: 53
Vib./Trem.: On, Small (Opt. Off)

13
Electronic Organs
Upper: String 8'
Lower: Flute 8', Reed 4'
Pedal: 16', 8' Medium Soft
Vib./Trem.: On, Full (Opt. Off)

Tonebar Organs
Upper: 00 4456 667
Lower: (00) 6332 221
Pedal: 52
Vib./Trem.: On, Full (Opt. Off)

4
Electronic Organs
Upper: Flutes (or Tibias) 8', 4', 2',
Reed 4'
Lower: Flutes 8', 4', Horn 8'
Pedal: 16', 8' Medium
Vib./Trem.: On, Full

Tonebar Organs
Upper: 00 8808 050
Lower: (00) 8880 000
Pedal: 62
Vib./Trem.: On, Full

14
Electronic Organs
Upper: Flute (or Tibia) 8',
Horn 4',
String 4'
Lower: Flutes 8', 4'
Pedal: 16', 8' Medium
Vib./Trem.: Off

Tonebar Organs
Upper: 00 8880 080
Lower: (00) 8800 000
Pedal: 54
Vib./Trem.: Off

5
Electronic Organs
Upper: Flutes (or Tibias) 8', 4', 2',
String 8'
Lower: Diapason 8', Reeds 8', 4'
Pedal: 16', 8' Medium Loud
Vib./Trem.: Off

Tonebar Organs
Upper: 00 8888 000
Lower: (00) 6655 554
Pedal: 55
Vib./Trem.: Off

15
Electronic Organs
Upper: Clarinet 8'
Lower: Flute 8', String 4'
Pedal: 16', 8' Medium
Vib./Trem.: On, Full (Opt. Off)

Tonebar Organs
Upper: 00 8282 805
Lower: (00) 6543 322
Pedal: 52
Vib./Trem.: On, Full (Opt. Off)

6
Electronic Organs
Upper: Full Organ 16', 8', 4', 2', 1'
(Brilliant)
Lower: Flutes 8', 4',
Strings 8', 4', Reed 4'
Pedal: 16', 8'
Medium Loud/Sustain
Vib./Trem.: On, Full

Tonebar Organs
Upper: 60 8080 887
Lower: (00) 7754 443
Pedal: 56 String Bass
Vib./Trem.: On, Full

16
Electronic Organs
Upper: Flutes (or Tibias) 8', 4'
Lower: Flute 8', Reed 4'
Pedal: 16', 8' Medium Soft
Vib./Trem.: On, Small (Opt. Off)

Tonebar Organs
Upper: 00 8008 000
Lower: (00) 6322 441
Pedal: 52
Vib./Trem.: On, Small (Opt. Off)

7
Electronic Organs
Upper: Flutes (or Tibias) 16', 8',
4', 2', 1'
Lower: Diapason 8', Flute 8',
String 8'
Pedal: 16', 8' Medium
Vib./Trem.: On, Small (Opt. Off)

Tonebar Organs
Upper: 60 8808 008
Lower: (00) 6656 543
Pedal: 54
Vib./Trem.: On, Small (Opt. Off)

17
Electronic Organs
Upper: Oboe (or Reed) 8'
Lower: Flute 8', String 4'
Pedal: 16', 8' Medium Soft
Vib./Trem.: Upper: Off
Lower: On

Tonebar Organs
Upper: 00 4685 421
Lower: (00) 5433 321
Pedal: 52
Vib./Trem.: Upper: Off
Lower: On

8
Electronic Organs
Upper: Flutes (or Tibias) 8', 2',
String 4', Reed 4'
Lower: Diapason 8' (Flute 8',
String 8')
Pedal: 16', 8' Medium
Vib./Trem.: Off

Tonebar Organs
Upper: 00 8008 555
Lower: (00) 6554 222
Pedal: 54
Vib./Trem.: Off

18
Electronic Organs
Upper: Full Organ 16', 8', 4', 2', 1'
Lower: Flutes 8', 4', String 8',
Reed 4'
Pedal: 16', 8' Medium Loud
Vib./Trem.: On, Full (Opt. Off)

Tonebar Organs
Upper: 60 8838 667
Lower: (00) 7654 332
Pedal: 65
Vib./Trem.: On, Full (Opt. Off)

9
Electronic Organs
Upper: Flutes (or Tibias) 8', 4', 2'
Lower: Clarinet 8' (or Flute 8',
Reed 4')
Pedal: 16', 8' Medium
Vib./Trem.: Off

Tonebar Organs
Upper: 00 8808 000
Lower: (00) 8080 400
Pedal: 52
Vib./Trem.: Off

19
Electronic Organs
Upper: Flutes (or Tibias) 16', 4',
Horn 8'
Lower: Diapason 8', String 8'
Pedal: 16', 8' Medium
Vib./Trem.: On, Full (Opt. Off)

Tonebar Organs
Upper: 80 0800 805
Lower: (00) 6554 221
Pedal: 54
Vib./Trem.: On, Full (Opt. Off)

10
Electronic Organs
Upper: Full Organ 16', 8', 4', 2', 1'
Lower: Flutes 8', 4', 2',
Strings 8', 4'
Pedal: 16', 8' Medium Loud
Vib./Trem.: On, Full (Opt. Off)

Tonebar Organs
Upper: 60 6666 666
Lower: (00) 7746 554
Pedal: 62
Vib./Trem.: On, Full (Opt. Off)

20
Electronic Organs
Upper: Flutes (or Tibias) 8', 1',
Reed 4' (Tierce)
Lower: Flute 8', String 4'
Pedal: 16', 8' Medium
Vib./Trem.: Off

Tonebar Organs
Upper: 00 8000 468
Lower: (00) 6322 222
Pedal: 54
Vib./Trem.: Off

GREAT ORGAN SELECTIONS

BIG BAND & SWING
Relive the dance hall days with this great collection of 25 swingin' favorites: All or Nothing at All • Ballin' the Jack • Basin Street Blues • East of the Sun • I Can't Get Started with You • I'm Beginning to See the Light • Manhattan • Mood Indigo • Old Devil Moon • Paper Doll • Route 66 • Sentimental Journey • Stormy Weather • Tenderly • Witchcraft • and more.
00199010 Organ $9.95

CHRISTMAS FAVORITES
80 Christmas classics every organist should know: Auld Lang Syne • Away in a Manger • Blue Christmas • Christmas Time Is Here • Dance of the Sugar Plum Fairy • The First Noël • Frosty the Snow Man • God Rest Ye Merry, Gentlemen • Have Yourself a Merry Little Christmas • I Saw Three Ships • It Came upon the Midnight Clear • Jingle Bells • Joy to the World • A Marshmallow World • O Holy Night • Rockin' Around the Christmas Tree • Silent Night • Up on the Housetop • What Child Is This? • White Christmas • and many more.
00144576 $14.99

CONTEMPORARY CHRISTIAN CLASSICS
12 songs of praise, including: El Shaddai • How Majestic Is Your Name • More Than Wonderful • Upon This Rock • We Shall Behold Him.
00199095 $6.95

GOSPEL TREASURES
35 gospel favorites for organ: Amazing Grace • Blessed Assurance • Higher Ground • I Love to Tell the Story • In the Garden • Just a Closer Walk with Thee • Nearer, My God, to Thee • The Old Rugged Cross • Rock of Ages • Shall We Gather at the River? • Sweet By and By • What a Friend We Have in Jesus • Wonderful Peace • and many more.
00144550 $7.99

LES MISÉRABLES
14 songs from Broadway's longest-running musical arranged for organ, including: At the End of the Day • Bring Him Home • Castle on a Cloud • Do You Hear the People Sing? • I Dreamed a Dream • In My Life • On My Own • and more.
00290270 $12.99

THE MOST BEAUTIFUL SONGS EVER
70 beautiful melodies arranged for organ: Autumn Leaves • Edelweiss • How High the Moon • If I Were a Bell • Luck Be a Lady • Misty • Ol' Man River • Satin Doll • Smile • Stardust • Summertime • Till There Was You • Unchained Melody • The Way You Look Tonight • Witchcraft • and more.
00144638 $16.99

105 FAVORITE HYMNS
Hal Leonard Organ Adventure Series – No. 18
arr. Bill Irwin
105 songs, including: Amazing Grace • The Church in the Wildwood • Holy, Holy, Holy • and more.
00212500 $10.95

THE PHANTOM OF THE OPERA
Nine songs from the Tony-winning Broadway sensation that every organist should know: All I Ask of You • Angel of Music • Masquerade • The Music of the Night • The Phantom of the Opera • The Point of No Return • Prima Donna • Think of Me • Wishing You Were Somehow Here Again.
00290300 $14.99

POP CLASSICS
24 Favorites Arranged for Organ
24 top hits, including: Can't Help Falling in Love • Daddy's Little Girl • Eleanor Rigby • Endless Love • Every Breath You Take • Hopelessly Devoted to You • Islands in the Stream • Let It Be • Mandy • Sea of Love • Unchained Melody • Woman in Love • Yesterday • You Needed Me • and more.
00199012 $9.95

SHOWTUNES
25 favorites from the stage to enjoy playing in your very own home! Includes: Bewitched • Blue Skies • Cabaret • Camelot • Edelweiss • Get Me to the Church on Time • Getting to Know You • I Could Write a Book • I Love Paris • Memory • Oklahoma • One • People • The Sound of Music • The Surrey with the Fringe on Top • Tomorrow • and more.
00199009 $9.95

SUNDAY SOLOS FOR ORGAN
Preludes, Offertories & Postludes
Contains 30 blended selections perfect for organists to play every Sunday: Abide with Me • El Shaddai • He Is Exalted • Holy Ground • Lamb of Glory • A Mighty Fortress Is Our God • Rock of Ages • Via Dolorosa • What a Friend We Have in Jesus • and more.
00199016 $12.99

WONDERFUL STANDARDS
Take a trip down memory lane with these 25 gems arranged for organ: After You've Gone • Ain't Misbehavin' • Autumn Leaves • Bluesette • Body and Soul • Dinah • The Girl from Ipanema • How Deep Is the Ocean • How Insensitive • I Should Care • I've Got You Under My Skin • My Favorite Things • My Romance • Red Roses for a Blue Lady • September Song • So Nice (Summer Samba) • Watch What Happens • Younger Than Springtime • and more.
00199011 $9.95

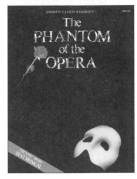

HAL•LEONARD® CORPORATION
7777 W. Bluemound Rd. P.O. Box 13819 Milwaukee, WI 53213

www.halleonard.com

Prices, contents, and availability subject to change without notice.